DATE DUE

D1378972

Aa • Bb • Cc • Aa • Bb • Cc • Aa • Bb • Cc • Aa • Bb • Cc • Aa • Bb • Cc

I Can Write My ABC's:
Quick & Creative Activities

by Kama Einhorn

Aa • Bb • Cc • Aa • Bb • Cc • Aa • Bb • Cc • Aa • Bb • Cc • Aa • Bb • Cc

SCHOLASTIC
PROFESSIONAL BOOKS

NEW YORK • TORONTO • LONDON • AUCKLAND • SYDNEY
MEXICO CITY • NEW DELHI • HONG KONG • BUENOS AIRES

For my letter-perfect friends, in alphabetical order:
Carolyn, **D**ave & **D**an, **E**ric, **E**rica & **E**sther, **J**ulie & **J**ana, **L**ucas,
Mimi, Mr. **O**, **R**aquy, **S**ue & **S**amantha, and the **X**-cellent Sadie Girl

Acknowledgments
*Grateful thanks to Liza Charlesworth and Terry Cooper for their
editorial consideration and guidance, to my thoughtful editor, Danielle Blood,
and to all my colleagues at Professional Books,
who make coming to work every morning a true pleasure.*

The activities in this book have been reviewed for safety and are meant to be done by children with adult supervision. The author does not assume any responsibility for injuries or accidents that might result from performing these activities without proper supervision and precautions.

Cover design by Jim Sarfati
Cover illustrations by Cheryl Phelps
Interior design by Solutions by Design, Inc.
Interior illustrations by James Graham Hale

ISBN: 0-439-22846-8

CONTENTS

INTRODUCTION

Welcome to *I Can Write My ABC's: Quick & Creative Activities*

It has been said that the invention of the alphabet is the single most important event in human civilization. What would our world be like without letters? These 26 abstract building blocks—each with its own unique arrangement of lines, curves, or dots—work together in endless combinations to represent ideas. We need to copy these forms clearly and consistently in order to record our thoughts on paper.

Children (and their teachers and parents!) take great pride in their first attempts at writing these forms. Learning letter formation is an important step on the road to becoming writers. When children feel comfortable and confident putting pencil to paper, they are more likely to enjoy the entire writing process!

With the creative, engaging, hands-on activities in this book, children will easily remember the shape of each letter as they develop into writers and readers. We hope you and your class enjoy the many adventures these 26 characters can provide!

Using This Book

This book includes dozens of engaging, multisensory activities to help children learn to recognize and write each letter, from *A* to *Z*. Each letter has its own page with a mnemonic rhyme that teaches each letter's formation; two creative, classroom-tested activities for introducing and reinforcing each letter; a fun fact about the letter; and a book link.

Mnemonic Rhymes help children (especially auditory learners) learn and remember letter formation. As you demonstrate how each letter is formed, read the rhyme aloud.

Activities involve all learning styles (see pages 6–7 for profiles of each learning modality). Two engaging ideas for teaching and reinforcing each letter are presented on each page. The following key will help you identify the activity's learning modality.

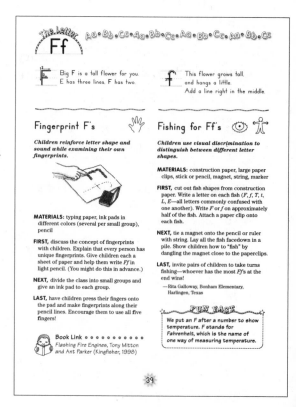

Auditory   learn by hearing

Visual   learn by seeing

Kinesthetic   learn by moving

Tactile   learn by touching

In addition:

 indicates a messy activity.

Book Links suggest specific books that highlight each target letter. These books are a great addition to a library corner or storytime area. Together, examine the book's cover and ask for a volunteer to find and point to the target letter. As you read the story with the group, you might ask a volunteer to point to the target letter on each page or to form the letter on chart paper. You might also ask a child whose name begins with that letter to be the page-turner.

Fun Facts enrich children's understanding of our alphabet system and language use. Share these bits of information with children as you introduce each letter.

In addition to the 26 letter-by-letter activity pages, you'll also find a section of Teaching Tips. Refer to this section on pages 6–12 for strategies on teaching to all learning styles, working with learning challenges, helping second-language learners, and more. Additional activities, ideas, and reproducible materials are provided on pages 13–32, including bulletin board ideas, whole alphabet activities, a reproducible ABC mini-book, and reproducible ABC stationery. On pages 60–63, you'll find a helpful list of recommended alphabet books to further enrich your letter studies—from *A* to *Z*!

TEACHING TIPS

How Children Learn Letter Formation

Most children learn to name and recognize the letters (usually uppercase) before they enter kindergarten. Recognizing and naming both upper- and lowercase letters, as well as practicing and refining the formation of these letters, is usually a new focus in kindergarten and first grade.

Uppercase letters are easier to distinguish visually, but lowercase letters are more commonly found in kindergarten and first-grade texts. Later, in second or third grade, children will face the additional challenge of recognizing four different forms of each letter: upper- and lowercase manuscript (print) and upper- and lowercase cursive. A solid foundation with manuscript letters will pave the way for future writing and reading success.

Students learn letter formation best through active exploration of letter names, the sounds the letters stand for, the letter's visual characteristics, and the motor movements involved in their formation (Bear et al., 1996). In this book, you'll find activities that integrate all these elements involved in letter recognition and formation.

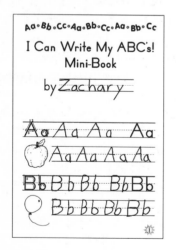

Teaching to All Learning Styles

You already know that there are a range of learning styles in your classroom: that visual learners learn best by seeing, tactile learners by touching, physical learners by doing, and auditory learners by hearing. You also know that these styles will continue to come into play as students learn to write.

You have probably also noticed that students do not fit into neat little boxes and that there is often an overlap between learning styles. Although these activities are grouped by learning style—visual, tactile, kinesthetic, and auditory—they are usually appropriate for the whole group. It is a good idea to give every child a chance to engage in all kinds of activities; combining modalities often leads to faster learning!

Visual Learners

Visual learners enjoy closely examining, copying, tracing, and highlighting letters. When provided with a clear written model, they are able to "imprint" that letter into their memory. These students might take naturally to traditional handwriting instruction, such as independently copying rows of letters. With their good visual memory and mental imaging strategies, visual learners often ease into writing without a great deal of explicit instruction.

Tactile Learners

Tactile learners learn best by incorporating their sense of touch into their letter-formation experience. These students will "key in" to a letter by exploring it through texture and shape. Physical interaction such as touching, tracing, and retracing letters is an effective strategy for tactile learners.

Kinesthetic Learners

For some learners, gross-motor (large muscle) movement is key to success, especially as they first experience a new letter. These are kinesthetic (or physical) learners, who learn new material best by involving their entire bodies. Air tracing or manipulating large letters, staying physically active as they create letters, and stretching their fingers before and after writing will help these learners.

Auditory Learners

Auditory learners need to hear information because they remember best what they hear and say. They benefit from memory strategies such as hearing a rhyme and then repeating it. Sound-symbol associations play a large role in their learning, as do describing and discussing letter forms, hearing short descriptions of how to form each letter, and taking oral directions as they write.

Working With Learning Challenges

For students with learning disabilities, it is most important to provide activities that fit a range of learning styles to compensate for limitations. A combination of tactile, kinesthetic, auditory, and visual activities nurtures different learning styles and involves the whole group.

Children with learning difficulties face many different issues in handwriting instruction. You may notice certain features of children's writing or learning process that cause concern. In these situations, refer children to a specialist for evaluation. (First be sure to rule out visual problems when considering children's learning issues.) The following are some of the disabilities that affect letter formation.

Dysgraphia, or the lack of control of handwriting muscles
Children with dysgraphia may:

* write backward.
* use heavy pressure, thereby smudging their paper.
* struggle to maintain consistent spacing within and between words.
* erase repeatedly.

Fine-Motor Limitations
Children with fine-motor difficulty face a particularly frustrating task in letter practice. These children may:

* struggle to control writing utensils and scissors.
* struggle to button and zip clothing.
* have difficulty copying simple shapes.

Visual Memory/Discrimination Weaknesses
Children with poor visual memory may:

* confuse letter orientation (for instance, *b* and *d*, *n* and *u*).
* reverse a series of letters (for instance, *saw* and *was*).
* confuse left with right, and over with under.

Auditory Processing Weaknesses
Children with poor auditory processing and memory may:

* struggle to follow a sequence of directions.
* reverse vowel-consonant combinations (such as *thrid* for *third*).

Do I need to adjust my teaching strategies for left-handed students?

If you are using practice sheets, left-handed students may be unable to see the model letter at the beginning of a practice line. Practice pages should include model letters at both ends of the line so that the model is always visible.

Aa • Bb • Cc • Aa • Bb • Cc • Aa • Bb • Cc • Aa • Bb • Cc • Aa • Bb • Cc

Working With Second-Language Learners

Newcomers to the United States may be familiar with English letter forms if their native language uses the Roman alphabet, but English letter names and sounds may be new to them. Children whose first language does not use the Roman alphabet will be learning letter shapes, sounds, and names simultaneously.

Early experience in letter-sound correspondence builds a solid vocabulary base for children. In addition, independently practicing rows of letters can actually be a relaxing, nonthreatening early school experience for children who are not yet speaking English.

Help second-language learners ease into letter formation and sound-symbol correspondence by:

✳ providing the child with an audiotape of the ABC song to listen to at home.

✳ repeatedly sharing the most basic alphabet books with the child.

✳ focusing on simple sound-symbol correspondence and showing clear pictures (for example, write "s is for *sun*" and show a simple drawing of a sun).

✳ inviting a family member to visit the class and demonstrate how letters of their alphabet are formed (if their first language uses a non-Roman alphabet). The group can then try their hand at forming these letters.

✳ inviting children to share their native language's version of the ABC song.

How should I assess children's handwriting?

Keeping a portfolio of each child's work throughout the year will allow you to provide a record of children's progress that is helpful to share with families during conferences. Keep in mind that the goals of handwriting practice are legibility and consistency. In order to be legible, a child's writing does not need to look exactly like the handwriting chart or like other children's writing. Instead, children should try to be consistent in their own writing so that each letter looks the same every time they write it.

Letter-Practice Procedures

The following four steps are a guide for introducing children to each letter.

1. Preview the letter on the board before having children write it. Teach the letter name first, so that children have a conceptual peg on which to hang their understanding. Slowly demonstrate each letter on the board as you read its mnemonic rhyme aloud. The mnemonic rhymes are located at the top of each letter-activity page.

2. Have students trace each letter in the air as you read the rhyme again.

Demonstrate how to do this by holding your thumb and first two fingers together, as if gripping a pencil, and forming the letter in the air.

3. Ask students to pick up their pencils and try to write one letter on their paper. Circulate around the room and check to see that children have understood the basic strokes. If they haven't, take their hand in yours and guide them through the strokes.

4. Invite children to complete one row of the letter and then circle their best letter in the row.

Materials

Medium-soft, standard-sized pencils are usually the most comfortable for children to use in practicing letters on paper. You may wish to give children small eraser tops before they begin letter practice, as lots of erasing with a dry or worn-out eraser can be frustrating. Although traditional handwriting instruction is done with paper and pencil, remember that writing in different mediums (crayons, markers, paint, pen, and so on) also helps reinforce letter formation. Standard white paper with top and bottom lines and a dotted middle line is recommended. (A dotted middle line in a different color is especially helpful.)

"Can I Sharpen My Pencil?"

It is tempting, especially for older children, to want to keep the sharpest point possible as they create their new letters. But the line for the pencil sharpener—and the noise of the sharpener—can be distracting!

Here are four easy management strategies for the "sharpener shuffle":

✹ Make pencil sharpening a morning ritual only. As children get settled, they should sharpen at least three pencils for the day's use.

✹ To cut down on line time and noise, provide two or more quiet electric sharpeners and put them in two corners of the room.

✹ When children go to the sharpener, have them sharpen several pencils at a time.

✹ Encourage children to sharpen their pencils at home.

Commonly Confused Letter Pairs

Children recognize letters by visually analyzing the shape and orientation of each letter. However, with so many similarities between letters, it is common for even third-graders to confuse certain letters. When presenting a pair of similar letters (for instance, *b* and *d*), be sure that children have already mastered one letter in the pair. This will eliminate additional confusion.

Use the following visual and auditory hints to help children discriminate between these letter pairs:

a-d *d* has his tail in the air, like a **d**og.

a-o Like an **a**pple, *a* has a stem. Like an **o**range, *o* does not.

b-d Have children hold their hands in front of them and form a *b* with their left hand and a *d* with their right. Move their hands together and help them see the "**bed**."

b-h *b* has a **b**all that **b**ounces; *h* has two legs that **h**op.

b-p and b-q *b* is like a **b**all that bounces up, so the line goes up, not down.

c-e *e* is just like *c*, but it has an **e**xtra **e**dge.

c-o *c*'s mouth is open to eat a **c**ookie. *o* is closed, like the shape of an **o**range.

d-q and g-q *q* has a fancy curl in its hair, like a **q**ueen.

d-g *g* goes down into the **g**round.

d-p *d* has a tail that stays above water, like a **d**uck. *p* has a round penny and a tail that goes down, like reaching down to put a **p**enny in your **p**ocket.

f-t *f* has a little **f**eather in his cap, but *t* has only a little **t**ip at the top.

g-p *g* has a tail that curls, like a **g**erbil's. *p*'s tail is straight, like a **p**ole.

h-n and h-u *h* goes up **h**igh.

p-q   *p* comes right before *q* in the alphabet, so the bat comes before the ball on *p*, and the bat comes after the ball on *q*.

u-v   *v* comes to a point, like a **v**alentine heart.

v-w   *v* looks like a **v**ampire's fang; *w* looks like **w**aves.

v-y   *y* is just like *v*, but it has a piece of **y**arn hanging down.

C-G   *C* is wide open, but *G* has a little **G**ate, or **G**arage, at its opening.

D-O   Big *O* is like a big **O**range.

E-F   *E* has an **E**xtra line.

I-J   *J* looks like *I*, but the bottom part of *J* **J**umps up a little.

I-L and **L-T**   *L* has a **L**ap!

K-X   *K* has a back and kicks out an arm and a leg, like a **K**arate **K**ick.

M-N   *M* looks like two **M**ountains.

M-W   *M* looks like two **M**ountains; *W* looks like **W**aves in the **W**ater.

O-Q   *Q* is holding his finger to his lips for "**Q**uiet!"

P-R   *P* and *R* look the same, but *R* has a **R**amp you can **R**ace down.

U-V   *U* is the c**U**p; *V* is the **V**ase.

V-Y   *Y* is like *V*, but it stands on a stick.

ALPHABET ACTIVITIES, IDEAS, AND REPRODUCIBLES

26 Alphabet Activities for Any Time

This section provides activities that can be used to introduce and reinforce any letter of the alphabet, or the alphabet as a whole. The letter-by-letter activities on pages 33–59 provide ideas for teaching each specific letter.

The ABC Song

Here are some of the many possible games and activities you can do with the familiar alphabet song (sung to the tune of "Twinkle, Twinkle, Little Star"):

✸ Give each child a letter on an index card. As you sing the ABC song together, have children hold up their letter as it is sung. Slow the song down to simplify the activity, or speed it up for a challenge!

✸ Give one child a pointer and invite him or her to point to each letter on your class alphabet frieze as the group sings.

✸ Divide the class into seven groups and give each group a chunk of the song to remember: *ABCD*, *EFG*, *HIJK*, *LMNOP*, *QRS*, *TUV*, and *WXYZ*. Have each group stand up and sing their part of the song in the appropriate order.

✸ Sing the song to a different tune.

✸ Sing the song in different ways—fast, slow, in low voices, in baby voices, and so on.

Alphabet Necklaces

For fine-motor practice, children can use alphabet cereal and string to make necklaces in the art center. Point out that only certain letters have holes that you can put a string through: *A*, *B*, *D*, *O*, *P*, *Q*, and *R*.

Bats and Baseballs

Help children see the similarities between letters by providing a visual reference of "bats and balls." As you introduce each letter, ask for a volunteer to point out the bat (straight line) and/or ball (round portion) in each letter. Discuss similarities and differences using these terms—for instance, "*b* and *p* both have baseballs, but *b* has a bat that points up, while *p* has a bat that points down." This helps children categorize features that are the same and contrast them with features that are different (Bear et al., 1996). You might also refer to the forms as "sticks and circles" or "lines and circles."

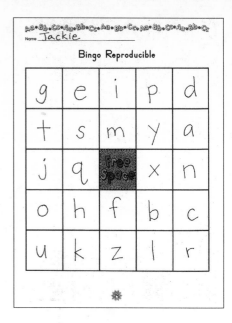

Bingo

Give each child a copy of the reproducible Bingo grid on page 19. Have children write a different letter (uppercase, lowercase, or both) in each empty space so that they write 24 different letters in all. Call out letter names (or describe how they are formed), and have children color in those squares. The first person to color five squares in a row wins.

Body Writing

Invite individuals or small groups of children to form letters with their bodies, either lying down or standing up. (Some letters, such as *R*, call for several children; other letters, such as *l*, can be formed by only one child.) Challenge the rest of the group to look at the formation and name the letter.

Chalkboard Practice

The chalkboard is ideal for beginning letter practice since writing on the board can be less tiresome on the hands and eyes. Children can look at the large letters at eye level and use gross-motor movements to write letters on the board. Handheld "line makers" are available in teacher supply stores and help you make practice lines quickly and evenly. You might also consider putting masking tape on the board to mark permanent practice lines.

Clay Tablets

Set up an ancient writing station! Tape a large sheet of foil or wax paper onto a desk or table. Flatten a large piece of soft clay into the shape of a tablet. Place the clay on top of the foil or wax paper and provide sticks or old pencils for writing utensils. Children can practice letters by carving them into the clay. Show them how to pat the clay down to erase!

Computer Fonts

Let children experiment on the computer with many fonts of the same letter. They might also play with size, color, italics, boldface, and so on.

Concentration

Write each upper- and lowercase letter on its own index card. (You will need 52 index cards in all.) Choose up to 12 cards (upper- and lowercase of six letters) and give them to children for a game of Concentration. To play, children place all of the cards facedown and take turns choosing pairs of cards to turn over. The object is to match uppercase letters to their lowercase versions.

Glitter Templates

Gather large index cards, a marker, glitter in different colors, yarn in two different colors, plastic straws cut into small pieces, scissors, and glue. With marker, write one letter on each index card (include top, bottom, and middle practice lines).

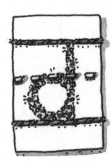

Distribute the cards evenly to children and invite them to create letter cards. Have them trace over the letter in glue and then sprinkle glitter on top. When the letter itself is dry, they should then glue yarn on the top and bottom line (using different colors for each), and glue the straw pieces on the dotted line. When the glue has dried, invite students to close their eyes and try to "read" one another's letters with their fingers. Have students feel the letter with their eyes open, then closed, and then open again. (You may wish to discuss the Braille alphabet with the group.) It is helpful to use these cards as new letters are introduced.

Index Cards

Index cards are a great resource for letter-recognition activities. Make and laminate a set of 26 cards, one for each letter.

✷ Give each child an index card with one letter on it. Invite children to sit in a circle. Play music and have children pass the cards in one direction around the circle. When the music stops, children name the letter on their card. For a fun variation, designate in advance one letter as the "hot potato." Explain that the student who holds the hot potato card during the final round will be the line leader the next day.

✷ Play a letter version of Simon Says. Hold up cards with the letters *Jj, Ww, Ss,* and have children jump when they see *Jj,* wave when they see *Ww,* or sit when they see *Ss.*

✷ Give each child a card with one letter on it. As children line up, chant, "Letter *A,* letter *A,* what comes next?" The children holding letters *A* and *B* line up, and then the group chants, "Letter *B,* letter *B,* what comes next?" Continue until the whole class has lined up.

✷ Line up the set of index cards in alphabetical order along the chalkboard ledge. Recite the alphabet in order, leaving out one or two letters. Ask children which letters you left out, and then remove those index cards from the board. Continue until there are no letters left.

I Spy

Look at the classroom alphabet frieze together. (It's best to display it at children's eye level.) Describe a letter. For instance, describe *O* by saying: "I spy with my little eye an uppercase letter that is perfectly round." Invite a volunteer to point to the correct letter on the alphabet frieze. Continue by describing other letters.

Jump Rope

The playground is a great place to practice letters! Have children play a large-group game of jump rope while they chant the alphabet, one letter for each jump. When a child misses a jump, he or she arranges the jump rope on the ground to form the letter on which the jump was missed.

Letter Bag

Gather resealable plastic bags and a tube of colored hair gel. (You can color clear gel with food coloring.) Give each child a plastic bag with a squirt of gel inside that is the size of a large marble. Help children seal the bags so there is no air trapped within. Then invite children to finger-trace letters onto this fun writing surface!

Letter Parade

Help children see that there are three different lowercase letter sizes: tall (*b, d, f, h, k, l, t*), small (*a, c, e, i, m, n, o, r, s, u, v, w, x, z*), and "underwater" (*g, j, p, q, y*). Write one letter on each of 26 index cards, shuffle the cards, and give one to each child. When it's time to line up, invite children to form a letter parade—tall letters first, then small, and then underwater. You might also challenge children to line up in alphabetical order within their size groups.

Line in the Sand

Gather sand, sticks, shells, coins, cut-up strips of old beach towels, and several large, flat, shallow plastic containers. (Shoe boxes work well but are less durable.) Create miniature sandboxes for the classroom by filling the container with sand. Add a little water to each box to make the sand damp enough to write in, like sand at the beach. Invite children to choose a writing utensil: their finger, a stick, or a pencil. Children can practice writing letters and short words in their sandboxes. Add shells or coins to each box for dotting *i*'s and *j*'s. Add the towel strips for crossing *t*'s!

London Letters

Place a strip of masking tape on the floor in the shape of a large letter. Have children examine the letter. Then invite them to hold hands and walk around the letter in a circle, singing these words to the tune of "London Bridge": "Walk around the letter ____, letter ____, letter ____. Walk around the letter ____, my fair lady." Fill in the blanks with the letter on the floor.

Magic Letters

Place a sheet of white paper on top of various magnetic or stencil letters. Have children use crayons or colored pencils to rub over the letters (similar to gravestone rubbing).

Manipulatives

Collect letter-shaped manipulatives, such as stamps, sponges, stencils, and letter magnets (they'll stick on most chalkboards). To provide tactile reinforcement of letter forms, encourage children to free-play with these manipulatives or include them in your writing or art center.

Name Games

Children's names are an ideal starting point from which to teach letter formation and recognition:

❋ Play Pat-a-Cake: Draw a circle to represent a cake on the board. Chant with the group: "Pat-a-cake, pat-a-cake, baker's man. Bake me a cake as fast as you can. Pat it and prick it and mark it with a [first letter of any child's name], and put it in the oven for [child's name] and me." Have the child write the first letter of his or her name inside the cake.

❋ Have children line up in alphabetical order by first or last names, from *Aa* to *Zz* or from *Zz* to *Aa*.

❋ When introducing a certain letter, have a child whose names begins with that letter demonstrate it for the group.

❋ Use children's names in transition times—for example, write a letter on chart paper and say, "Whoever has this letter in their name may line up."

Paper Chains

Give each child a strip of colored construction paper. Have children each practice writing one letter all over their strip. (There should be 26 different letter strips when finished.) Help children staple the strips into links to form an alphabet chain—*Bb* attaches to *Aa*, *Cc* attaches to *Bb*, and so on.

Skywriting

Ask one child to stand with his or her back to the group. Have the child trace a large letter in the air with his or her finger while the group guesses the letter. Invite children to take turns "skywriting" letters.

Tongue Twisters

As you introduce a letter, emphasize the letter-sound connection by writing an alliterative sentence on the board. Ask a volunteer to circle all the beginning letters with the same sound. For instance, a child would circle six *S*'s in "Silly Sammy spins and slips on a spilled smoothie."

White Boards

Have individual children practice and erase letters on small write-on, wipe-off white boards. This is helpful for children who erase repeatedly.

Write Back

Use your finger to draw a letter on one child's back, letting the rest of the group see what you are doing. Have the child guess the letter you wrote. Children can also play this game in pairs.

Zany Writing

Help children focus on the shapes and lines of letters written in bright, engaging colors. Set out fluorescent highlighters and metallic markers (available in gold, silver, and copper from stationery or art stores). Invite children to practice letters on unlined, white paper. They may do this in any way they like. Model the technique of writing in a fluorescent color and then tracing the outline of the letter in a metallic hue (or vice versa).

Name _____   Date _____

Bingo Grid

		Free Space		

Food Clues

Before you introduce each letter, give each student a small, nonmessy piece of food. Before they eat the food, ask children to guess which letter they'll be practicing that day. Additionally, you might use a handful of the food to form the letter itself and then share it with the group.

Aa: almonds, apricots, animal crackers

Bb: banana slices, banana chips, blueberries

Cc: chocolate chips, cherries, carrots

Dd: dates, doughnuts

Ee: eggs (or chocolate eggs wrapped in foil)

Ff: figs, Fig Newtons™

Gg: grapes, Gummi Bears™, gumdrops, goldfish crackers

Hh: honey (a drop on each child's finger)

Ii: ice cubes (Pass one around the room for children to hold, not to eat.)

Jj: jellybeans, Jell-O™ cubes

Kk: kisses (chocolate), kiwi slices

Ll: lemon drops, licorice, Lifesavers™

Mm: M&M's™, mini-marshmallows

Nn: mixed nuts, nectarine slices

Oo: Oreos™, orange wedges, oatmeal cookies

Pp: pear slices, potato chips, popcorn, pretzels

Qq: any food arranged in the shape of a *Q* or *q*, or fruit cut into quarters

Rr: raisins

Ss: sunflower seeds

Tt: tangerine wedges, Twizzlers™

Uu: any food that children can hide **u**nder their desks!

Vv: valentine hearts

Ww: walnuts, Gummi Worms™, small chunks of watermelon

Xx: licorice or pretzel sticks arranged in an X

Yy: yogurt, small pieces of cooked yam

Zz: zucchini bread or cooked zucchini slices

Safety Note:
Be sure to check with families about any food allergies children may have.

Bringing the ABC's to Your Bulletin Boards

Seeing print all around your classroom will help improve children's visual memory. Add colorful letters to your bulletin boards to enrich the classroom environment and build alphabetic awareness.

The Alphabet Garden

Cover a bulletin board with a green background. Staple a strip of green corrugated bulletin board border along the bottom for grass. Add the title "Alphabet Garden" or "How Does Your Garden Grow?" Have children cut out pictures of flowers in magazines and add them to the garden. In the garden, display a row of 26 paper flowers. To make the flowers, cut out a circle from construction paper for the middle of each flower. Then attach colored tissue paper behind the circle for petals. As you teach each letter, write or paint the letter on a flower. Eventually, you will "grow" an alphabetical row of flowers!

Alphabet Soup

Cut out a large semicircle from craft paper for the bowl and staple it onto a colorful background. Attach table props, such as paper or cloth napkins, a checkered tablecloth, a menu, a chef's hat, and so on. Explain to children that as they learn each letter, you'll add the letter to the alphabet soup until the whole alphabet is ready to eat. Staple cut-out letters to the bowl. You might also staple children's letter art or practice sheets. When all 26 letters are in the bowl, celebrate by making and eating real alphabet soup!

Alphaquilt

As children learn each letter, have them take turns adding a decorated letter square to a paper quilt. Use different-colored squares of construction paper and staple each square onto the bulletin board as it is created. The quilt should be five squares wide and five squares tall. For the 26th letter, add *Q* as part of the title "Our Alphabet **Q**uilt."

Letter Caterpillar

Cut out a circular caterpillar's head from colored paper and staple it to one end of a long bulletin board. As you teach each letter, have children take turns making and decorating a letter circle to add to the caterpillar. If you have more than 26 children in your class, ask some children to make letter circles for a title, such as "Our ABC Caterpillar."

Underwater ABC's

Cover three-quarters of a bulletin board with blue craft paper or blue cellophane for an underwater effect. Cut the top of the paper so that it looks like waves. Attach pictures of sea creatures on the blue paper. Glue sandpaper for sand on the ocean floor. Attach 26 cut-out construction paper letters along the top of the mural, "above water." (Or attach index cards with a letter written on each.) As you teach each letter, invite a volunteer to move the letter "underwater." When the group has learned all 26 letters, all letters will be underwater. Add the title "Dive into the Alphabet!"

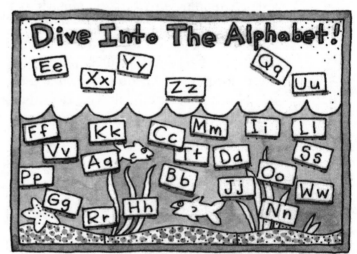

Alphabet Treasure

Cut out a large treasure chest from colored craft paper. Attach it to the center of a bulletin board. Glue scraps of sandpaper around the chest for a sandy effect. Cut out 26 circles from yellow paper for coins. As you introduce each letter, have children take turns writing the letter on a coin and decorating the letter with glitter. Staple the letter coins in the treasure chest.

Teaching With Alphabet Books

Alphabet books provide many teachable moments as children are learning letter formation. On pages 60–63, you'll find an extensive list of suggested alphabet books to share with your students. Here are some ways to enhance the reading experience:

* Assign each child a letter to remember. As you read each letter page, ask the child with that letter to write it on chart paper, turn the page, or point to the letter on the page.

* Compare the first letters of children's names to the corresponding page in the alphabet book.

* Have children guess which letter will be on the next page.

* Skip a page now and then to see if children can identify which letter's page you skipped.

* Sing the ABC song together as you turn the pages quickly, rather than reading the book.

* Try finding things on each page that begin with the letter featured on the page.

Make-Your-Own Alphabet Books

Children can make their own illustrated alphabet books by taking eight sheets of unlined, $8\frac{1}{2}$ by 11-inch white paper, putting them in a neat pile, folding the pile in half, and stapling the folded edge. This provides a page for each letter, a front and back cover, "The End" page, and a dedication page. Invite children to create thematic alphabet books by drawing animals, school, food, sports, and so on.

The alphabet mini-book on pages 29–32 can be used as a letter-practice activity. Make double-sided copies of the pages so that page 2 appears behind page 1, and page 4 appears behind page 3. Fold the pages, arrange them in order, and staple along the spine. Invite children to refer to their mini-book when singing the alphabet song.

Sign Language Letters

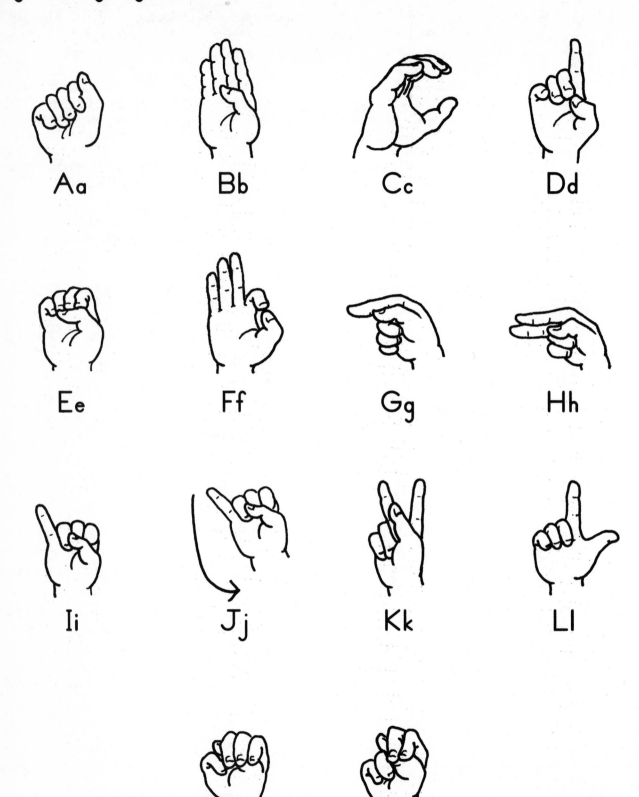

Aa   Bb   Cc   Dd

Ee   Ff   Gg   Hh

Ii   Jj   Kk   Ll

Mn   Nn

Sign Language Letters

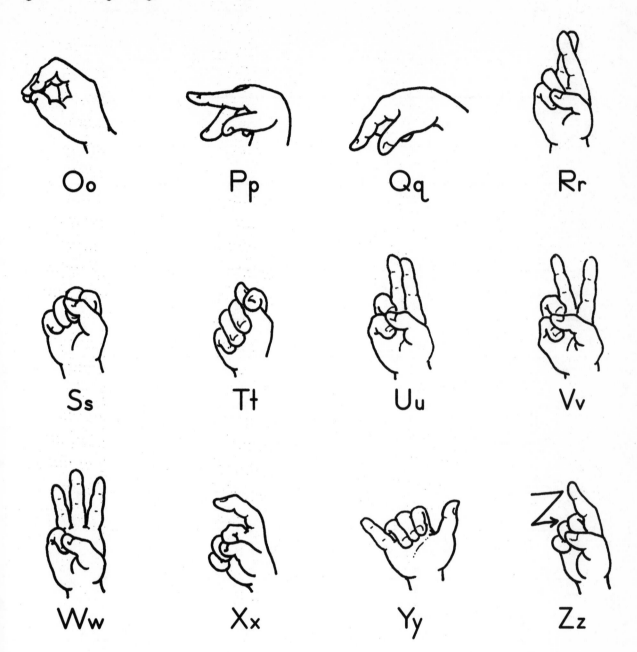

Oo   Pp   Qq   Rr

Ss   Tt   Uu   Vv

Ww   Xx   Yy   Zz

Aa

Bb

Cc

Dd

Ee

Ff

Gg

Hh

Ii

Jj

Kk

Ll

Mm

Nn

Oo

Pp

Qq

Rr

Ss

Tt

Uu

Vv

Ww

Xx

Yy

Zz

Now that I know my ABC's,
Here's a letter to you from me!

ABCDEFGHIJKLMNOPQRSTUVWXYZ

abcdefghijklmnopqrstuvwxyz

I Can Write My ABC's! Mini-Book

by _____

Aa

Bb

Xx

Yy

Zz

Now I know my ABC's.

Next time won't you sing with me?

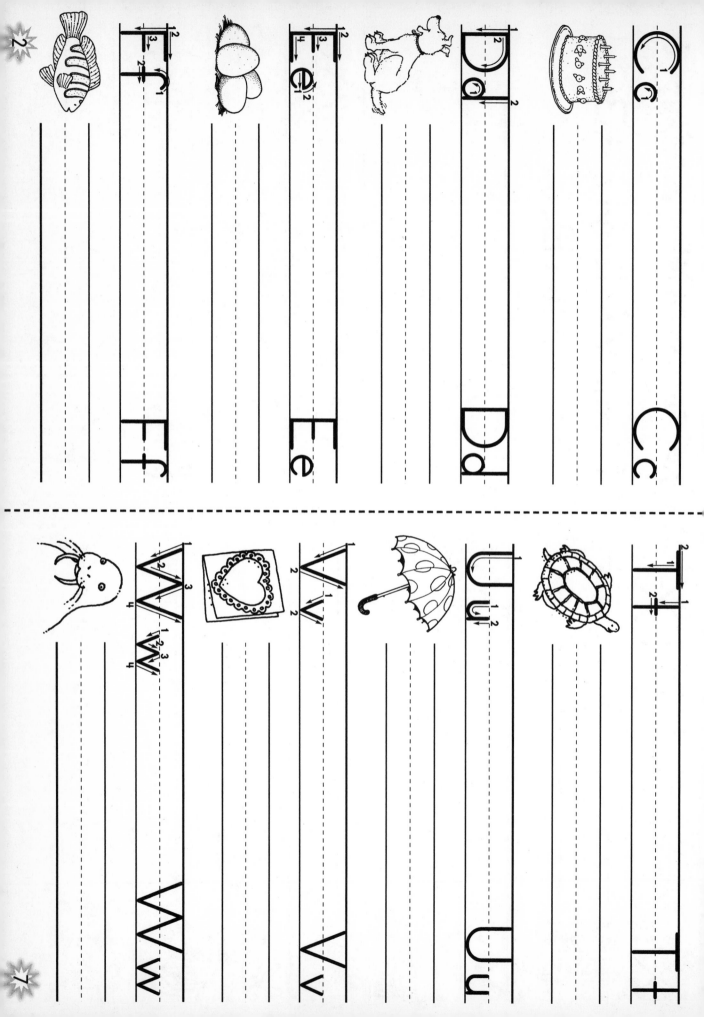

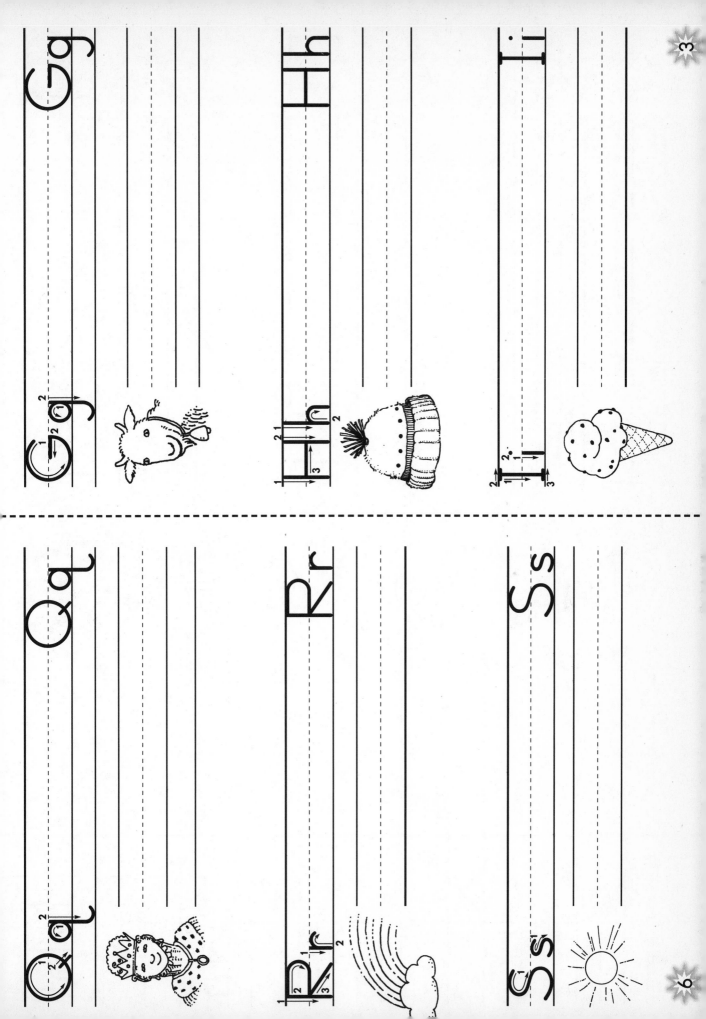

Gg

Hh

Ii

Qq

Rr

Ss

Letter-by-Letter Activities

 Pull down twice
from the point at the top.
Add a seat to view the apple crop.

 First make a round apple to eat,
then a slide for an ant
when he's finished his treat!

Apple A's

Students form the letter Aa in a sweet-smelling activity.

MATERIALS: apples (1 per child), cloves (a handful per child), ribbon or yarn, permanent marker

Safety Note: *Be sure to tell children not to eat the cloves. Also tell them not to eat the finished apple ornament since it will have marker on it.*

FIRST, give each child an apple and a handful of cloves. Help children write an *A* and *a* on their apple in thick lines with permanent marker. Write the uppercase *A* on one side of the apple and the lowercase *a* on the other. (You might do this for children in advance.)

NEXT, invite children to push the cloves into the apples in the shape of *A* and *a*, using the lines as a guide. Help children tie a ribbon or piece of yarn around the stem so they can hang it as an ornament.

LAST, children can take their apples home to use as an ornament or give as a gift—a scented letter *Aa*!

 Book Link ✳ ✳ ✳ ✳ ✳ ✳ ✳ ✳ ✳
Angry Arthur, Hiawyn Oram
(Harcourt Brace Jovanovich, 1982)

A Is for...

Children identify short and long Aa sounds as they form letter shapes.

MATERIALS: handfuls of small items beginning with *Aa*: apricots, almonds, acorns, animal crackers, dried apple chips, Apple Jacks™, plastic ants, small address stickers, autumn leaves, and so on

FIRST, sit with children in a circle and display all *Aa* objects. Have children guess what the objects have in common. Point out that *Aa* has two different sounds, long and short. Explain that long vowels say their name, as in *acorn*. As a group, sort the objects into two piles: short *Aa* and long *Aa*.

NEXT, ask for a volunteer to arrange one type of object into an upper- and lowercase *Aa* in the middle of the circle.

LAST, repeat with each different object.

— Debbie Rovin-Murphy, Richboro Elementary, Richboro, Pennsylvania

 ☆ **FUN FACT** ☆
The expression "from A to Z" means "from beginning to end."

Bb

 Big old **B** has a tall straight back, and two big bellies 'cause he just ate a snack!

 Draw a straight back, just like me. Don't forget to add a belly for **b**!

Baby Blueberry-Banana Bites

Children identify sound-symbol correspondence with a healthy snack.

MATERIALS: bananas ($\frac{1}{2}$ per child), plastic knives (1 per child), blueberries (a handful per child), toothpicks (1 per child), blue permanent markers, paper towels or napkins

FIRST, give each child a paper towel or napkin and blue marker or crayon. Invite them to practice writing a large *B* and *b* on their napkin or paper towel. (You might have them line up their blueberries along the lines of their letters.)

NEXT, help students cut their bananas and make banana-blueberry "kebabs" on their toothpicks.

LAST, eat and enjoy! As children eat, ask them to think of other foods that begin with *Bb* and make a list on chart paper.

 **FUN FACT**

In ancient times, this letter was called "bet."

 Book Link ✳ ✳ ✳ ✳ ✳ ✳ ✳ ✳ ✳
Baby Beebee Bird, Diane Redfield Massie (Harper & Row, 1963)

Who's Got the Button?

Children use their sense of touch to explore the shape and orientation of Bb.

MATERIALS: buttons (in various shapes, sizes, and colors), oaktag (2 sheets per child), pencils, glue

FIRST, gather children around you to examine the buttons. This is a good opportunity to discuss classification and attributes.

NEXT, help children trace *B* and *b* with pencil on oaktag, one letter per sheet. Have them estimate how many buttons they will need to cover their *Bb*'s. Help them put glue on the letters and add buttons to form the shape of *B* and *b*. Let dry.

LAST, play a tactile letter-recognition game. There are two ways to play: The first way is to have one child hold the *b* right-side up. Another child holds the *b* upside down, so the *b* looks like *q*. A third child closes his or her eyes and feels both letters. If the *b* is right-side up, the child says "_____'s got the button," filling in the blank with the name of the child holding the *b*. The second version is to have two children hold up their letters: one with *B* and the other with *b*. A third child closes his or her eyes, feels the letters, and identifies the uppercase and lowercase letters.

—Debbie Rovin-Murphy, Richboro Elementary, Richboro, Pennsylvania

Cars can cruise down curvy c.
Stop near the ground—
that's it, you see!

Confetti C's

Children reinforce the shape of Cc in a fun medium.

MATERIALS: confetti (store-bought or homemade), construction paper (1 sheet per child), pencils, glue, cotton swabs

FIRST, explain that machines make confetti by cutting up different colors of paper into small pieces. Ask children when confetti is used. Point out that *confetti* and *celebration* begin with Cc. Brainstorm other party-oriented words such as *cookies, carnival, clown,* or *cake.*

NEXT, give children each a sheet of construction paper and have them write their best *Cc*'s in pencil. Help them use cotton swabs to cover their pencil lines with glue.

LAST, help children sprinkle confetti over the glue and shake off the excess. After the glue has dried, invite children to close their eyes and feel the letters. (You might try the same activity with cotton instead of confetti.)

FUN FACT

Big *C* and little *c* are twins, except for their size.

C Is for Cookie

Children use their sense of touch and taste to explore and enjoy the letter Cc.

MATERIALS: store-bought chocolate chip cookie dough, cookie sheet, tinfoil, oven

FIRST, show children the *C*'s on the package of cookie dough. Separate the chilled dough into small balls. Have children wash their hands, and then give each child a ball of dough on a piece of tinfoil.

NEXT, invite children to roll out their dough into long ropes on their tinfoil. Then have each child form letter *Cc*'s on their foil and place them on a cookie sheet. (If dough becomes too sticky, let children dust their hands with a bit of flour.) Write children's initials on the edge of the foil, several inches from the dough. Bake according to the directions on the package.

LAST, enjoy the cookies together. Sing "*C* is for Cookie" before you eat, or listen to the song on tape as you enjoy the snack!

—Shelly Nitkin, Radburn School, Fair Lawn, New Jersey

Book Link ✷ ✷ ✷ ✷ ✷ ✷ ✷ ✷ ✷
Cat's Colors, Jane Cabrera
(Dial Books for Young Readers, 1997)

 Down to the ground,
then take a break.
Half a circle is what you'll make.

 First you make a dime to spend.
Go way up high,
then down to the end.

Dot-to-Dot D's

Children build fine-motor skills as they form the shape of **Dd** *again and again.*

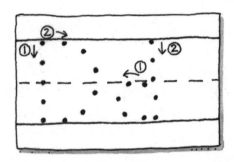

MATERIALS: laminator, erasable markers, white paper, pencils

FIRST, in advance, draw dot-to-dot *Dd*'s in marker on white paper. Laminate the sheets to make write-on/wipe-off practice sheets.

NEXT, show children the sheets and point out that the *Dd*'s are made of dots. Let children use erasable marker to connect the dots and form the *Dd*'s. They can wipe off their lines when finished and try again.

LAST, children can use paper and pencil to create their own dot-to-dot letters—*Dd* or any other letter—for their classmates to complete.

 Book Link * * * * * * * * * * *
The Day the Dog Said, "Cock-a-doodle-doo!", David McPhail (Scholastic, 1996)

Duck Walk

Children form the letter **Dd** *with their bodies and distinguish between upper- and lowercase letters.*

MATERIALS: cassette player and upbeat music

FIRST, have children crouch down and hold on to their ankles. When they try to walk, they will look like ducks! Tell half the group to pretend they are baby ducklings and the other half to pretend they are mama or papa ducks.

NEXT, play music and invite children to do the duck walk! When the music stops, have children find a partner. Ducklings should pair with other ducklings, ducks with other ducks. Each pair of ducklings lies down and forms a *d* on the floor; each pair of mama or papa ducks forms a *D*. Have children observe one another's formations.

LAST, vary the activity by having children move like dogs, dinosaurs, dragons, dodo birds, or dolphins!

—Shelly Nitkin, Radburn School,
Fair Lawn, New Jersey

 **FUN FACT**

We put a *d* sound at the end of a verb to show it happened in the past: *Yesterday I walked to school.*

Ee

Pull straight down for capital E. Then add some shelves. 1, 2, 3.

A little line starts off **e**. Add a plate for an egg— here's breakfast for me!

Eggshell Sidewalk Chalk

Children create a new writing utensil for gross-motor writing practice.

MATERIALS: 6 washed and dried eggshells, 1 tsp. hot water, 1 tsp. flour, a drop of food coloring, blender, strainer or sifter, bowls, measuring spoons, paper towels

FIRST, ask children to bring in clean, dry eggshells from home. (Or ask a local restaurant to save their eggshells one morning.)

NEXT, use a blender to grind the eggshells into a powder. Sift the powder into a large bowl, keeping out any large pieces of eggshell. Mix together the eggshell powder, water, flour, and food coloring.

LAST, shape the mixture into a large piece of chalk and roll it tightly in a paper towel. Let it dry in a warm, dry place for two to three days. Children can then use the eggshell chalk to practice writing *Ee*'s and other letters outside on a playground surface or on the sidewalk!

FUN FACT

E is the most commonly used letter in the alphabet!

An E for Everybody

*Students form a whole-class **E** as they explore sound-symbol correspondence.*

MATERIALS: sidewalk chalk (you might use the recipe at left), playground surface

FIRST, have children help you draw a large *E* on the playground surface. The letter should be about 10 to 20 feet high, depending on your class size. Have children stand off to one side and examine the shape.

NEXT, ask each child to name something that begins with *Ee* (*everybody, extra, egg, earth, eye, edge,* and so on). Once they do, ask them to stand on the line of the *E*. If children have trouble thinking of words, you might give them clues such as "You eat this for breakfast." Or invite children to contribute words with an *e* sound in them, such as *me, bee, free,* and so on.

LAST, after each child has named a word, you will have a large *E* shape. This is a nice photo opportunity! Repeat with lowercase *e* or any other letter.

—Jennifer Levin Boss, Oakridge Elementary, Hollywood, Florida

Book Link ✳ ✳ ✳ ✳ ✳ ✳ ✳ ✳ ✳ ✳
Engine, Engine, Number Nine, Stephanie Calmenson (Hyperion, 1996)

Big F is a tall flower for you.
E has three lines. F has two.

This flower grows tall,
and hangs a little.
Add a line right in the middle.

Fingerprint F's

Children reinforce letter shape and sound while examining their own fingerprints.

MATERIALS: typing paper, ink pads in different colors (several per small group), pencil

FIRST, discuss the concept of fingerprints with children. Explain that every person has unique fingerprints. Give children each a sheet of paper and help them write *Ff* in light pencil. (You might do this in advance.)

NEXT, divide the class into small groups and give an ink pad to each group.

LAST, have children press their fingers onto the pad and make fingerprints along their pencil lines. Encourage them to use all **five** fingers!

 Book Link ✳ ✳ ✳ ✳ ✳ ✳ ✳ ✳ ✳ ✳
Flashing Fire Engines, Tony Mitton and Ant Parker (Kingfisher, 1998)

Fishing for F's

Children use visual discrimination to distinguish between different letter shapes.

MATERIALS: construction paper, scissors, large paper clips, ruler or pencil, magnet, string, marker

FIRST, cut out fish shapes from construction paper. Write a letter on each fish (*F, f, T, t, L, E*—all letters commonly confused with one another). Write *F* or *f* on approximately half of the fish. Attach a paper clip to each fish.

NEXT, tie a magnet onto the pencil or ruler with string. Lay all the fish facedown in a pile. Show children how to "fish" by dangling the magnet close to the paper clips.

LAST, invite pairs of children to take turns fishing—whoever has the most *Ff*'s at the end wins!

—Rita Galloway, Bonham Elementary, Harlingen, Texas

FUN FACT

We put an F after a number to show temperature. F stands for *Fahrenheit*, which is the name of one way of measuring temperature.

Gg

 Big round circle,
but don't go too far.
Add a garage to park your car!

 A garden starts with a little seed.
The roots grow down.
That's all you need!

How Does Your Garden Grow?

Children plant their own letters and watch them appear!

MATERIALS: alfalfa seeds, foil cake pans (1 for each child), soil, spray bottle for watering

FIRST, in advance, poke a few small holes in the bottom of each cake pan and put an inch of soil into each pan. Ask children to think of things that begin with *Gg*, such as *garden*, *gardener*, *grow*, *green*, and *grass*.

NEXT, give each child a pan. Ask children to trace either *G* or *g* in the soil with their index finger. Then have them drop seeds evenly into the groove of the letter.

LAST, place the pans on top of newspaper in a sunny spot. Let children spray the soil lightly with water every day. Check the pans daily for signs of growth and enjoy the green *Gg*'s!

Gooey, Gluey G's

Children form Gg's with glue.

MATERIALS: squeeze containers of colored glue (in various colors), wax paper (one square per child)

FIRST, ask children to name words that start with *Gg*. Mention *glue*, *gooey*, and *glop*!

NEXT, invite children to form *G* and *g* on their wax paper with the glue. Let the glue dry. (For extra fun, sprinkle some glitter on each letter before it dries!)

LAST, help children peel their gluey *Gg*'s off the wax paper. Have children stick the *Gg*'s in various places. Like Colorforms™, these *Gg*'s will stick to a white board and many other smooth surfaces!

In Greek, *G* is called gamma.

 **Book Link** ✱ ✱ ✱ ✱ ✱ ✱ ✱ ✱ ✱ ✱
Good Night, Gorilla,
Peggy Rathmann (Putnam, 1994)

 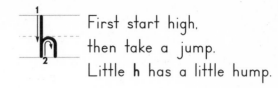

Make two lines, high to low.
Connect the lines
so they can say hello!

First start high,
then take a jump.
Little **h** has a little hump.

Honey Writing

Children practice forming the letter Hh in a sweet medium.

MATERIALS: tinfoil (1 square per child), honey in squeeze containers (1 per small group), masking tape

FIRST, have children wash their hands. Give each child a square of tinfoil and tape it to the desk or table. Give each small group a plastic honey dispenser.

NEXT, invite children to take turns squirting out the shapes of upper- and lowercase *Hh* onto their foil sheets.

LAST, children can eat their letters with their fingers! Alternatively, children can dip apple or orange slices into their letters for a healthy snack.

Helping Hands

Children create a whole-class mural in the shape of Hh.

MATERIALS: White craft paper, tempera paints in different colors, paper plates, pencil

FIRST, draw a large *H* and *h* in outlined letters on craft paper as children watch. (Or you might write *Helping hands* and outline the letters *H* and *h*.)

NEXT, put a little tempera paint on each paper plate. Have children dip one hand in the paint color of their choice.

LAST, have children take turns putting their colorful handprints all over the *H* and *h* until the letters are filled with helping hands!

—Jennifer Levin Boss, Oakridge Elementary, Hollywood, Florida

Hh can be silent, as in *Sarah*.

Book Link ✳ ✳ ✳ ✳ ✳ ✳ ✳ ✳ ✳
The Hat, Jan Brett
(Putnam, 1997)

Big I starts
with one side of a door.
All it needs
is a roof and a floor.

Little i goes down.
It's an ice cream treat.
Add a sprinkle on top
and it's ready to eat!

I Is for Ice Cream!

Children whip up a letter treat as they practice writing Ii.

MATERIALS: container of whipped cream, maraschino cherries (1 per child), sprinkles, tinfoil (1 square per child), permanent marker, masking tape

FIRST, have children wash their hands. Tell children that they are going to make *Ii* ice cream sundaes! Distribute tinfoil and tape it to desks or tables. Help children write *I* and *i* on the tinfoil with permanent marker (or you might do this in advance). On each child's foil sheet, place a maraschino cherry and a scoop of whipped cream (about the size of a tennis ball).

NEXT, ask children to spread out the whipped cream with their hands all over the foil until it forms an even layer. Invite them to use their fingers to trace *I* and *i* in the cream surface—the marker lines will show through when they are on the right path. Have children dot their *i*'s with their cherries! When finished, they can smooth out the surface and repeat.

LAST, when children have practiced for a while, shake some sprinkles onto their "ice cream sundae"! Children can then lick their fingers.

Icicle I's

Children form chilly letters at eye level.

MATERIALS: ice cubes, chalkboard, paper towels

FIRST, Write *Ice* and *ice* on the board. (You might write and discuss words that contain *ice* such as *ice cream, icicle, iceberg, Iceland, ice box, ice skate.*) Divide the class into small groups. Give each group an ice cube and some paper towels. Ask a child from each group to stand at the board.

NEXT, children can take turns forming *Ii*'s on the board, using their ice cubes as writing utensils. Encourage them to form *Ii*'s in all different sizes.

LAST, challenge children to choose their best *Ii* before the water dries!

—David Jefferies, Brandeis-Hillel Day School, San Francisco, California

☆ **FUN FACT**

Lowercase *i* and *j* are the only two letters that use dots.

Book Link ✳ ✳ ✳ ✳ ✳ ✳ ✳ ✳ ✳ ✳
Inch by Inch, Leo Lionni
(I. Obolensky, 1960)

 Jumping Jack J
jumps down and then curls up.
Jack needs a hat
'cause he likes to dress up!

 Little j is so thin and lean.
Jump way down,
then add a jellybean!

Jiggly J's

Children make and eat jiggly J's!

MATERIALS: letter-shaped cookie cutters (be sure *J* is included), 2 cups boiling water, two 8-ounce packages flavored gelatin, such as Jell-O™ (any flavor), large bowl, 13- by 9-inch pan

FIRST, stir boiling water into the gelatin mix in large bowl for 3 minutes or until the gelatin mix is dissolved. Pour the mixture into the pan and refrigerate for three hours.

NEXT, dip the bottom of the pan in warm water for about 15 seconds. Use cookie cutters to cut out as many *J*'s as you can, then any other letters children wish. Lift the letters from the pan.

LAST, enjoy the jigglers while sharing "*J*" tongue twisters, such as "Jeremy's jiggly Jello jumped out of his hand and into the jam jar!"

 Book Link ❀ ❀ ❀ ❀ ❀ ❀ ❀ ❀ ❀ ❀
Jamberry, Bruce Degen
(Harper & Row, 1983)

Jumping Jack J's

Children respond physically to the shape of a letter and rapidly discriminate between similar letters.

MATERIALS: seven index cards labeled *J, j, I, i, g, L,* and *T*

FIRST, sit with children in a circle. Show all the cards and see if children can name each letter. Have one child point out the *J* and *j* and put the two cards together.

NEXT, have children crouch very low. Show them one of the cards. If it's a *J* or *j*, they jump up like a jack-in-the-box. If it's not *J* or *j*, they do not.

LAST, speed up the activity for a challenge! Children might also enjoy leading this game.

—David Jefferies, Brandeis-Hillel Day School, San Francisco, California

FUN FACT

J was not even considered a letter in English until the 1800s. People used *i* and *y* instead.

The Letter Kk

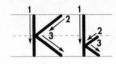

K and k have three lines,
as you can see:
a tall straight back,
and a sideways v.

Kaleidoscope K's

Children use keys to create colorful letter shapes.

MATERIALS: keys (1 per child), white paper, crayons in different colors

FIRST, discuss kaleidoscopes with children, sharing one if possible. Tell children they are going to use keys to "unlock" their own colorful "kaleidoscope *Kk*'s"! Invite children to use crayons to cover their paper with different colors, as heavily as they can.

NEXT, ask children to color over their colored paper with black crayon, again as heavily as possible.

LAST, give each child a key and show them how to scratch out the shape of *Kk*. Encourage them to scratch out very thick letters to reveal lots of color!

FUN FACT

K stands for Kindergarten!

Karate Kicks

Children use their whole bodies to form the letter **Kk.**

MATERIALS: a karate belt (or a sash or ribbon), index cards, markers.

FIRST, write the following letters on index cards, one per card: *K, k, X, x, I, t, V, v.* (Children often confuse these letters.) Discuss karate with children and ask one volunteer to wear the karate belt.

NEXT, show children a *K* and *k*. Point out that they each have a straight back, and a leg and an arm that do "karate kicks"! Ask the child wearing the belt to stand in front of the group and hold up the index cards one by one. Have the other children spread apart from one another. When they see a *K* or *k*, they use their left arm and leg to do a karate kick in the air!

LAST, speed up the activity for a challenge. Children may also hop like kangaroos instead of karate kicking.

—Kia Brown, PS 78, New York, New York

 Book Link ✳ ✳ ✳ ✳ ✳ ✳ ✳ ✳ ✳ ✳
A Kente Dress for Kenya,
Juwanda G. Ford
(Scholastic, 1996)

Pull down a line and add a lap.
Lie down, lazy!
It's time for a nap.

Little I looks like a number one.
Just draw a line,
and you are done!

Looking for Lemon L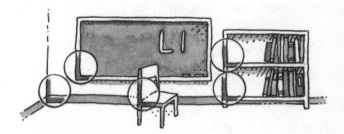

Children use invisible ink to form and examine letters.

MATERIALS: lemon juice in a small bowl, cotton swabs, blank white paper (1 sheet per child), an iron, 1 brown paper grocery bag

FIRST, invite students to dip their cotton swabs into the juice and, with the juice, write an *Ll* on the blank paper. (Have younger children simply watch as you demonstrate.) Let dry.

NEXT, sandwich children's papers between a folded paper grocery bag and rub with a medium-hot iron.

Safety Note: *Supervise children closely around the iron, and place the iron in a safe place while it is cooling.*

LAST, watch the *Ll*'s appear!

FUN FACT

In Chicago, Illinois, the subway is called the L, for "elevated railroad" because it is high up off the ground.

The L's Are Lost

Children examine the classroom environment for the lines of an **L.**

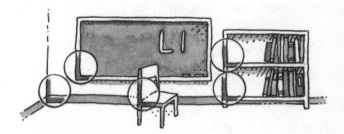

MATERIALS: none

FIRST, write *L* and *l* on the board. Tell children that there are many lost uppercase *L*'s in the room that they need to find!

NEXT, explain to children that since *L* is formed by two straight lines that come together, there are *L*'s all over the room. Point out several *L* formations: where the wall meets the floor, the corner of the chalkboard, the edges of the door, and so on. Invite children to explore the room looking for *L* formations.

LAST, have children sit down together and take turns showing the group where they found *L*'s.

—Jennifer Levin Boss, Oakridge Elementary, Hollywood, Florida

 Book Link * * * * * * * * * *
Leo the Late Bloomer,
Robert Kraus (Windmill Books, 1971)

Go down, hit the ground,
then draw a V.
Down to the ground again,
big **M** is two mountains for me.

Go down, hit the ground,
then get ready for bumps.
Little **m** is easy to write,
just add two humps.

Mirror, Mirror

Children explore the concept of letter symmetry and orientation.

MATERIALS: small mirrors, paper, pencils

FIRST, have children practice a row of uppercase *M*'s on paper.

NEXT, ask children what they think the *M*'s would look like in a mirror.

LAST, have children hold up their mirrors to the paper. Ask children why they think the letters in the mirror look exactly the same! What if the mirror were held at the halfway point of the *M* (between the two "mountains")? What other letters would look exactly the same if a mirror were placed at the halfway point? (*Oo, A, H, I, l, Tt, Uu, Vv, Ww, Xx,* and *Y.*) For younger children, you might simply demonstrate this as children observe.

FUN FACT

Mm goes up and down the mountain twice. (Try singing "The M Went Over Two Mountains" to the tune of "The Bear Went Over the Mountain.")

Mmmmm!

Children practice letter formation in different tasty mediums.

MATERIALS: mustard and mayonnaise (each in a plastic squeeze bottle), permanent markers, wax paper or tinfoil, masking tape, sandwich meat or crackers

FIRST, give each child a square of wax paper or tinfoil. Help them write *M* and *m* in permanent marker (you might do this in advance). Tape the squares to desks or tables. Divide the class into groups of four and give each group a bottle of mustard or mayonnaise. Have groups take turns using the different bottles. Ask children to find the *Mm*'s on the containers before they move on to the next step.

NEXT, invite children to squeeze the mustard or mayonnaise onto their letter lines to form *Mm*'s.

LAST, give children each a slice of sandwich meat or some crackers to dip into their *Mm*'s and eat!

—Megan Banta, St. Maria Goretti, Westfield, Indiana

Book Link ✳ ✳ ✳ ✳ ✳ ✳ ✳ ✳ ✳
To Market, to Market,
Anne Miranda
(Harcourt Brace, 1997)

Stick a nail in the ground,
and slant another one right.
Add a third pointing up,
and say nighty-night!

Go down, hit the ground,
and you're almost done.
Little m has two humps,
n has only one.

Noodle Writing N's

Children distinguish between straight and curved lines and describe the difference between uppercase and lowercase Nn.

MATERIALS: dry spaghetti noodles, cooked spaghetti noodles (rather than cooking, simply soak some in water overnight), sheets of newspaper (1 per child)

FIRST, give each child several dry spaghetti noodles. Challenge children to form an *N* on their newspaper.

NEXT, give each child several cooked noodles. Challenge children to form an *n* on their newspaper.

LAST, discuss the difference between raw and cooked noodles. Ask: *In what ways was working with the cooked noodles easier? In what ways was it harder? How many pieces of spaghetti did you need for each letter, and why?*

Book Link ✱ ✱ ✱ ✱ ✱ ✱ ✱ ✱ ✱
Noisy Nora, Rosemary Wells
(Dial Press, 1973)

FUN FACT

On a map or compass, N means "north."

A Nose for News

*Children identify **Nn**'s within dense text.*

MATERIALS: newspaper (with print on it as well as pictures), thin markers

FIRST, give each child a marker and a large sheet of newspaper. (This is a nice activity to do after the noodle activity.) Tell them they are going to pretend they are reporters with "a nose for news"!

NEXT, challenge children to find and circle as many upper- and lowercase *Nn*'s on their page as they can.

LAST, have children count their *Nn*'s to see who has the most. Repeat with any other letter.

—Megan Banta, St. Maria Goretti,
Westfield, Indiana

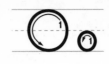

Oh, yum! An orange to eat!
Nice and round,
it's a healthy treat.

Big O and Little O

Children compare and contrast the size of upper- and lowercase Oo.

MATERIALS: various types of *O*-shaped cereal (such as Oh's™, Froot Loops™, Honey Bunches of O's™, and Cheerios™), colored construction paper (1 sheet per child), pencils, glue, cotton swabs

FIRST, give each child several handfuls of different cereals and a sheet of colored construction paper. Examine the cereal together and discuss how to separate it into two groups: big *O*'s and little *o*'s. Ask: *Which cereal is the smallest? Which is the biggest?*

NEXT, invite children to write an upper- and lowercase *Oo* in pencil on their paper. Then have them use cotton swabs to trace over the lines with glue.

LAST, have children glue the smaller *o* cereal pieces onto the lines of the lowercase *o* and the larger *O* cereal pieces onto the lines of the uppercase *O*.

FUN FACT

O can stand for hugs; XOXO means "kisses and hugs."

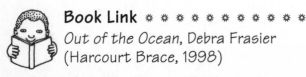

Book Link ✷ ✷ ✷ ✷ ✷ ✷ ✷ ✷ ✷ ✷

Out of the Ocean, Debra Frasier (Harcourt Brace, 1998)

The O-lympics

Children physically interact with round shapes.

MATERIALS: P.E. equipment (varies according to which games you choose to play), the plastic top of a six-pack of soda (1 per child), tinfoil, ribbon

FIRST, write *Olympics* on the board and discuss the Olympics with children. Point out that it begins with *O*. Discuss games children could play that start with *O* or games that involve round objects. Some might be:

✻ Hula hoop contest (Who can hula the longest? Or, who can step the quickest through hula hoops placed on the ground?)

✻ Orange-rolling (Whose orange rolled the farthest?)

✻ Soapy bubble-blowing contest (Who blew the largest bubble?)

✻ "*Oo*" scavenger hunt (Who can find the most *O*-shaped objects in the classroom?)

✻ An opposites matching game

NEXT, plan and play a class *Oo* Olympics!

LAST, make "*O*" Olympic medals to wear. Wrap tinfoil around the plastic top of a six-pack (so that it looks like an Olympic symbol), and tie a long piece of ribbon so children can wear it as a necklace. Ask: *How many O's are in your necklace?*

—Mary Jane Banta, Northeastern Elementary, Fountain City, Indiana

Pull down your pencil.
Then pick it up off the ground.
Add half a penny, nice and round.

Pop on down
and then up, you see.
Finish it off with a little pea!

Pink and Purple P's

Children make and use their own pink and purple writing utensils.

MATERIALS: old, broken pink and purple crayons, muffin tins (enough for 1 muffin compartment per child), spray cooking oil, oven, white paper, spoon

FIRST, spray the muffin tins with cooking oil and preheat the oven to 200 degrees. Have children peel the paper off the pink and purple crayons (point out all the *P* words in this sentence!).

NEXT, have children break apart the crayons into small pieces and put a handful into each muffin compartment. Place the pans in the oven and leave until the crayons have melted. Remove the pans from the oven. You might give each "muffin" a few stirs for a swirled effect. Let cool.

Safety Note: *Do not let children near the oven or hot pan.*

LAST, after the plastic has completely cooled, invite children to practice writing *P* and *p* on paper with their new crayons!

Book Link ✳ ✳ ✳ ✳ ✳ ✳ ✳ ✳ ✳ ✳
Pete's a Pizza, William Steig, (HarperCollins, 1998)

Peanut Butter Playdough

Children use their sense of taste, smell, and touch as they form the letter **Pp.**

Safety Note: *Be sure to ask families about children's allergies to any of the ingredients listed below.*

MATERIALS: 1 cup peanut butter, 1 cup instant nonfat dry milk, 2 T. honey, wax paper (1 square per child), wooden spoon

FIRST, mix together all the ingredients. Form one ball per student. Place the dough balls on wax paper and chill in the refrigerator.

NEXT, have children wash their hands. Then, give each child a ball of dough on a square of wax paper. Invite children to roll their dough into thin strips and form upper- and lowercase *Pp*'s on their wax paper.

LAST, invite children to eat and enjoy the peanut butter *Pp*'s!

—Mary Jane Banta, Northeastern Elementary, Fountain City, Indiana

FUN FACT

The expression "Mind your *p*'s and *q*'s" may have come from the 1700s, when teachers warned students not to get these letters mixed up!

 Big **Q** is a round quarter to spend.
Add a line when you're at the end.

 A fancy queen
with a little pearl.
Give **q**'s hair a special curl.

Quiet Quilt Q's

Children create a group quilt as they practice the letter Qq.

MATERIALS: white paper squares (all the same size, 1 per child), masking tape or clear tape, crayons, markers

FIRST, designate a place in the room as a quiet area. Give each child a paper square.

NEXT, point out that *quilt* begins with *q*. Explain that children are going to decorate their squares and then put them together to make a "quiet quilt" for a quiet place in the classroom. Have children write *Qq* on their square and decorate it however they like with crayons and markers.

LAST, arrange all squares facedown in a square grid and tape them together. (If you wish to hang the quilt, place the squares facedown and tape them together with masking tape. If you are not going to hang the quilt, place the squares faceup and tape them together with clear tape.) Point out that just as the squares of a quilt are sewn together, *q* and *u* are always together in words!

 FUN FACT

In English words, *q* is always followed by *u*.

Quill Writing

Children practice the letter Qq with an unusual writing instrument.

MATERIALS: craft feathers (1 per child, available at craft stores or teacher supply stores), manila paper (1 sheet per child), pencil, tempera paints on paper plates

FIRST, let children feel the feathers. Explain that quills, which are the hard tips of the feathers, were once carved out and filled with ink. They were used for writing before there were pens.

NEXT, ask children to write *Q* and *q* lightly with pencil on their paper.

LAST, have children gently brush the feathers through the paint and onto the paper. They should try writing with both ends of the quills. Let dry and then display them.

 Book Link ✲ ✲ ✲ ✲ ✲ ✲ ✲ ✲ ✲ ✲
The Keeping Quilt, Patricia Polacco (Simon & Schuster, 1988)

The Letter Rr

 Aa • Bb • Cc • Aa • Bb • Cc • Aa • Bb • Cc • Aa • Bb • Cc

First draw a line
and then a rainbow.
Add a ramp and you're ready to go!

Go straight down,
then race on back.
r has an arm, like a little rack.

Ring Around the R

Children develop letter-name and sound-symbol awareness as they form a giant human Rr.

MATERIALS: masking tape or playground chalk

FIRST, mark off a very large *R* and/or *r* with masking tape on the floor or with playground chalk outside.

NEXT, gather children in a circle and walk around the *Rr*, singing (to the tune of "Ring Around the Rosie") "Ring around the *R*. Ring around the *R*. Letter *R*, letter *R*, we all fall down!"

LAST, instead of falling down, each child rushes to sit on the lines that form the letter until the group has created a large human *R* or *r*!

FUN FACT

People used to say that school was for teaching the "Three R's": reading, 'riting and 'rithmetic! (Ask children which of these is the only one that really begins with R.)

 Book Link ✳ ✳ ✳ ✳ ✳ ✳ ✳ ✳ ✳
Little Red Riding Hood, retold and illustrated by Trina Schart Hyman (Holiday House, 1986)

Roller Coaster Races

Children use hand-eye coordination to maneuver their way around letter forms with a magnet.

MATERIALS: 2 small paper clips, 2 thin aluminum cookie sheets or tins, permanent marker, 2 strong magnets

FIRST, draw a roller coaster on each cookie sheet with marker, integrating the letters *R* and *r*, as shown. Have children play this game in pairs.

NEXT, give each child a cookie sheet and a magnet. Place the paper clips at the beginning of the roller coaster. Show them how to place the magnet under the cookie sheet and make their paper clips move around the lines of the roller coaster.

LAST, invite pairs of children to have roller coaster races—lowercase *r* against uppercase *R*!

—Rita Galloway, Bonham Elementary, Harlingen, Texas

 Silly S and s, those slithery snakes. Twisty, turny, ready to shake!

Sand Painting S's

Children create and decorate S's in a fun medium.

MATERIALS: pencils, sand, shells, glue, cotton swabs, construction paper

FIRST, help children write *Ss* in pencil on their construction paper. Then have them squeeze glue onto the letters (cotton swabs may make this easier).

NEXT, help children shake a small amount of sand onto the glue. Children might also use shells to decorate their *Ss*'s, or draw a sun on their paper. Shake off the excess sand and let the letters dry.

LAST, invite children to close their eyes and feel their sandy *Ss*'s!

FUN FACT

To turn an S into the number 8, all you need to do is add another backward S on top of it!

Soft, Slippery, Sandy S's

Children practice tracing S's on a variety of surfaces.

MATERIALS: shaving cream, 2 cups of salt, 2 cups sand, 2 cups soap flakes, 1 shell, 4 cookie sheets

FIRST, place salt in the first cookie sheet, soap flakes in the second, sand and the shell in the third, and a squirt of shaving cream the size of a tennis ball in the last sheet. Create four stations around the room, each with a cookie sheet.

NEXT, divide the class into four groups. Invite each group to visit a station where they can take turns finger-tracing *Ss*'s in the various mediums. (Provide a model letter on the board.) Have the groups rotate from station to station.

LAST, challenge children to finger-trace different letters and short words in the pans.

—Susan Anderson, IPS 81, Indianapolis, Indiana

 Book Link ✳ ✳ ✳ ✳ ✳ ✳ ✳ ✳ ✳
Sassafras, Audrey Penn (Child & Family Press, 1995)

Big T is a big tall tree.
Add a fort at the top
so you can see.

Little t is a little tree.
Add a fort in the middle
for you and me!

T for Two

Children discriminate between upper- and lowercase forms of Tt and distinguish between similar letters.

MATERIALS: several tambourines and/or triangle instruments, 6 index cards, marker

FIRST, write one letter on each index card: *T, t, F, f, l, I*. Then introduce the word *tiptoe* and demonstrate tiptoeing. (You might share the song "Tiptoe Through the Tulips.") Give several students tambourines or triangle instruments. Explain that they will be the "big *T*'s" and the other children will be the "little *t*'s."

NEXT, show children the index cards, one by one. When you show *T*, have the "big *T*'s" make a "big" sound with their instruments. When you show *t*, have the "little *t*'s" quietly tiptoe toward you. Show the cards randomly and speed up the pace for a challenge.

LAST, when all the "little *t*'s" have reached you, have the pairs switch roles and repeat the activity.

FUN FACT

Coaches or referees put their hands together in the shape of *T* to mean "Time out!"

Teatime T's

Children form Tt in a variety of tea grains.

MATERIALS: different types of loose tea (about 1 cup of each type, available in specialty coffee stores), shoe box lids

FIRST, discuss tea with children. Point out that the word *tea* sounds just like the letter's name! Let children smell the various types of tea you've brought in.

NEXT, place roughly 1 cup of loose tea in a thin, even layer in each shoe box lid.

LAST, have children finger-trace *T* and *t* in the grains of tea. Afterward, you might make tea for a tea taste test and graph children's favorites.

—Mitzi Fehl, Poquoson Primary School, Poquoson, Virginia

Book Link ✽ ✽ ✽ ✽ ✽ ✽ ✽ ✽ ✽ ✽
A Trio of Triceratops, Bernard Most (Harcourt Brace, 1998)

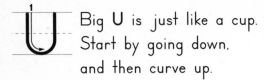

The Letter Uu

Big **U** is just like a cup.
Start by going down.
and then curve up.

Curve down and up,
then down once more.
Little **u** is a cup
that's ready to pour.

My Uncle's Unicorn

Children trace Uu's as they identify sound-symbol correspondence.

MATERIALS: chart paper, marker, metallic silver or gold marker (available in craft or stationery stores)

FIRST, discuss unicorns with the group. Mention that unicorns are magical, made-up creatures. Ask: *What do you know about unicorns?*

NEXT, write the following song in large letters on chart paper and read it to children.

My uncle has a unicorn, unicorn, unicorn.
Usually his unicorn
sleeps under the moon.

LAST, tell children that the song needs a little "unicorn magic" before it can be sung. Invite one or more children to use the "magical" marker to trace over all the *Uu*'s in the song, so that they are gold or silver. Then sing the song together to the tune of "Mary Had a Little Lamb."

Book Link ✱ ✱ ✱ ✱ ✱ ✱ ✱ ✱ ✱ ✱
Ugh, Arthur Yorinks
(Farrar Straus Giroux, 1990)

U and Me

Children use a hand rhyme to reinforce the shape and orientation of Uu.

MATERIALS: none

FIRST, have each child sit with a partner. One child should sit in front with his or her back facing the other child. Model this hand rhyme for the whole group:

Creating a *U* is easy to do.
Make a *C* for you to view
(Hold up hand in the shape of a *C*).

Turn it up for something new.
(Turn hand up in the shape of a *U*.)

What is it? *U!*

NEXT, invite the children sitting in the front to say the rhyme and do the hand movements. Ask the children in back to practice drawing *Uu*'s on their partner's back.

LAST, partners switch places.

—Mitzi Fehl, Poquoson Primary School, Poquoson, Virginia

FUN FACT

Sometimes people use Uu to stand for you.

 ♡ U = I love you!

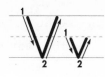
 Slant down first,
then up, like so.
This upside-down volcano
is ready to blow!

Very Vanilla V's

Children practice writing Vv on a yummy writing surface.

MATERIALS: 2 same-sized vanilla beans (available in specialty food stores or the spice section of the supermarket), tinfoil (1 square per child), masking tape, about 6 cups of vanilla pudding, permanent markers

FIRST, show the vanilla beans to the group. Pass them around so that children can smell them. Discuss how vanilla is used as a flavor (you might show a bottle of vanilla extract as well). Ask: *Why do we have two vanilla beans as we learn the letter* V, *rather than one or three?* Lay the beans out in the shape of *V*. Then pick them up and ask for volunteers to take turns forming *V* with the vanilla beans.

NEXT, have children wash their hands. Distribute tinfoil and help children write a *V* and a *v* with permanent marker on the tinfoil (you might do this in advance). Tape the foil to desks or table surfaces and put a large spoonful of pudding on each child's square. Invite children to spread the pudding into a very thin layer using their fingers.

LAST, children can use their fingers to write *Vv*'s on their vanilla writing surface (the guiding marker lines will show through). Afterward, they can lick their fingers (or dip in 'Nilla Wafers™ for an extra treat)!

 Book Link ✳ ✳ ✳ ✳ ✳ ✳ ✳ ✳ ✳ ✳
The Velveteen Rabbit, Margery Williams (Doubleday, 1960)

Vegetable Prints

Children form Vv's with vegetables and paint!

MATERIALS: large sheet of craft paper, zucchini, yellow squash, onion, broccoli, cucumbers, potatoes, knife, tempera paint in different colors on small paper plates, pencils

FIRST, examine the produce with the group. Ask: *What do all these have in common?* Guide children to understand that all of these things are vegetables. Have children watch as you cut the vegetables in preparation for printing. (With the exception of broccoli, cut vegetables so that a flat surface is exposed. Dry off any moisture. Cut the broccoli into small florets. You might also do this in advance.)

NEXT, invite children to write a large *Vv* in pencil on craft paper. Have them choose a vegetable, dip the cut surface into paint, and print along the lines of *Vv*. Children can make a *Vv* with each different vegetable.

LAST, have children paint green vines all over their vegetable mural!

—Kia Brown, PS 78, New York, New York

FUN FACT

If you hold up your index finger and your middle finger, you can make a "victory" sign.

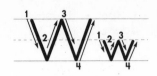

W and w have two pointy waves. Swim in the water if you're brave!

Water Writing

Children practice writing with gross-motor movements in a wet medium.

MATERIALS: sponges in different shapes and sizes, water, classroom chalkboard

FIRST, distribute sponges to children and invite them to wet their sponges. Point out that *water* and *wet* both begin with *w*. This is a good opportunity to wash the chalkboard!

NEXT, have children practice upper- and lowercase *Ww*'s on the board with their wet sponges. The sponges will darken the board so that children can see their writing.

LAST, encourage children to choose their best *w* before the water dries! Children can try writing with different types of sponges.

FUN FACT

W is a good letter for asking questions: Who? What? When? Where? and Why?

 Book Link ✳ ✳ ✳ ✳ ✳ ✳ ✳ ✳ ✳ ✳
A Whistle for Willie,
Ezra Jack Keats (Viking, 1964)

Windcatchers

Children practice letter formation on decorative objects that reinforce letter-sound connection.

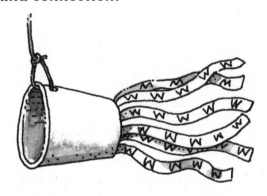

MATERIALS: long strips of colored tissue paper (about 11 inches by 1 inch, up to 10 per child), empty, clean pint-size ice cream containers (1 per child), masking tape, markers, hole punch, string

FIRST, discuss wind with children (*wind* starts with *Ww*, and also sounds a little bit like *www*). Distribute the colored tissue paper (children may want to choose their colors).

NEXT, have children practice *Ww*'s with markers all over their tissue paper.

LAST, help children tape their tissue strips onto the smaller end of their ice cream container (cut out the bottom first). Punch a hole in the ice cream container and attach string so windcatchers can hang outdoors.

—Susan Anderson, IPS 81, Indianapolis, Indiana

 A criss and a cross,
and in case you forgot,
where is the treasure?
X marks the spot!

Tic-Tac-Toe

Children play a popular game while practicing letter forms.

MATERIALS: chalkboard or paper and pencils

FIRST, help children pair off. Show children how to make a tic-tac-toe grid and teach them how to play tic-tac-toe.

NEXT, invite pairs of children to play tic-tac-toe using *Xx*'s and *Oo*'s. You might let them choose between "uppercase tic-tac-toe" and "lowercase tic-tac-toe."

LAST, challenge children to play using different letter pairs, especially ones that children commonly confuse (see pages 11–12).

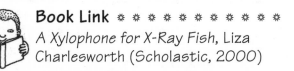

Book Link ✸ ✸ ✸ ✸ ✸ ✸ ✸ ✸ ✸ ✸
A Xylophone for X-Ray Fish, Liza Charlesworth (Scholastic, 2000)

An X-cellent Snack

Children make edible Xx's while focusing on the letter's line orientation.

MATERIALS: any number of the following: miniature pretzel sticks, licorice sticks, Gummi Worms™, carrot sticks, celery sticks, french fries, bread sticks, strips of American cheese

FIRST, have children wash their hands. Then show children an *X* on chart paper or the board. Distribute a handful of each type of food to each student at desks or tabletops.

NEXT, have children form as many *X*'s as they can with their materials. You might distinguish between upper- and lowercase *Xx*'s by designating licorice for the uppercase *X*'s and pretzel sticks for the lowercase *x*'s.

LAST, invite children to eat and enjoy their edible *Xx*'s as you share this rhyme: "*X* is in *excited,* and oh how excited are we! We make a crisscross for an *X* and eat it, you and me!"

—Barbara Hipple, Immaculate Conception, Levittown, Pennsylvania

FUN FACT

People say "X marks the spot" because pirates used to bury treasure and mark the spot on a map with an X.

Capital Y has a V in the air.
The pole at the bottom
holds it there.

 Slant down right,
down to the ground.
Slant down left,
and take it underground.

Yummy Y's

Children practice letter formation on an edible surface while reinforcing sound-symbol correspondence.

MATERIALS: several small containers of yogurt in any flavor, tinfoil squares (1 per child), masking tape, permanent marker

FIRST, have children wash their hands. Distribute foil and help children write a *Y* and *y* on their tin foil sheets with permanent marker (you might also do this in advance). Tape the sheets onto desks or tables. Show children the letter *Y* on the yogurt container. Place a large spoonful of yogurt on each child's square.

NEXT, invite children to use their hands to spread the yogurt into a very thin layer covering their foil. They can then practice writing *Y* and *y* with their index fingers right on their yummy writing surface. The guiding lines will show through as they follow the correct letter path.

LAST, children can lick their fingers!

FUN FACT
Y is the only letter that is both a vowel and a consonant.

We're Y's!

*Children form the letter **Y** with their bodies and use this form as a model for writing practice.*

MATERIALS: pencils, paper

FIRST, show children an uppercase *Y* on the board or chart paper. Invite everyone to stand up.

NEXT, say, "Now let's make the letter *Y*. Stand straight and tall, hands up to the sky!" Children hold up their arms so that their bodies form giant *Y*'s.

LAST, invite one child to stand in front of the group and model the letter as children practice writing *Y*'s on paper.

—Barbara Hipple, Immaculate Conception, Levittown, Pennsylvania

 Book Link * * * * * * * * * *
Yoko, Rosemary Wells
(Hyperion, 1998)

Zigzag Z and z are easy, you see.
Just zig a zag—1, 2, 3!

Zippity Z's

Children play with the Zz sound as they form the letter in a familiar song.

MATERIALS: chart paper, black marker

FIRST, Write *Zz* on chart paper and point out that you are using black marker on a white piece of paper. Ask: *Which animal has black and white stripes?* Have children name other things that are black and white. Invite students to make the "zzz" sound. Ask: *What does it feel like in your mouth?*

NEXT, write the lyrics to "Zippity Doo-Da" on chart paper, leaving out the *Z*'s. Invite a volunteer to write them in for you. Explain that *zippity* is a nonsense word.

Zippity doo-da, zippity day
My, oh my, what a wonderful day.
Plenty of _____ coming my way,
Zippity doo-da, zippity day!

LAST, have children sing together, substituting a *Zz* word in the blank (such as *zippers*, *zebras*, *zeros*, *zoos*, *zigzags*, *zinnias*, and *zip codes*).

FUN FACT

"Zzz" is sometimes written to show the sound people make when they are snoring!

Book Link ✳ ✳ ✳ ✳ ✳ ✳ ✳ ✳ ✳ ✳
The Z Was Zapped, Chris Van Allsburg (Houghton Mifflin, 1987)

Zip a Z

Children interact with each line of the letter Z in a specific sequence and direction.

MATERIALS: zippers (3 per child, found at fabric or craft stores), pencils, sturdy colored poster paper (1 small sheet per child), glue

FIRST, have children write a *Z* in pencil on their paper. Distribute zippers (all three should be roughly the same size, though one could be longer than the other two). Explain that children will form a *Z* with their zippers. Ask: *Why do you think you need three zippers and not two or four?*

NEXT, have children glue their three zippers onto their three lines (one per line, so that the zipper unzips in the direction in which your pencil would move if you were writing it). Supervise closely to help children glue only the edges of each piece down, rather than the metal part. Let dry.

LAST, say the mnemonic rhyme at the top of the page aloud and have children zip or unzip their zippers on "1, 2, 3."

—Barbara Hipple, Immaculate Conception, Levittown, Pennsylvania

Alphabet Books

Alphabet Books

ABC by Jan Pie'nkowski (Little Simon, 1998)

ABC by William Wegman (Hyperion, 1994)

ABC Animal Riddles by Susan Joyce (Peel Productions, 1999)

The ABC Bunny by Wanda Gag (Coward, McCann & Geoghegan, 1978, © 1933)

ABC Dogs by Kathy Darling and Tara Darling (Walker & Co., 1997)

ABC: Egyptian Art From the Brooklyn Museum by Florence Cassen Mayers (Harry N. Abrams, 1988)

ABC Yummy by Lisa Jahn-Clough (Houghton Mifflin, 1997)

Abracadabra to Zigzag: An Alphabet Book by Nancy Lecourt (Lothrop, Lee & Shepard, 1991)

A, B, See! By Tana Hoban (Greenwillow, 1982)

A, My Name Is Alice by Jane Bayer (Dial Books for Young Readers, 1984)

A You're Adorable by Buddy Kaye (Candlewick Press, 1994)

The Absolutely Awful Alphabet by Mordicai Gerstein (Harcourt Brace, 1999)

The Accidental Zucchini: An Unexpected Alphabet by Max Grover (Browndeer Press, 1993)

Afro-Bets ABC Book by Cheryl Willis Hudson (Just Us Books, 1988)

Alfred's Alphabet Walk by Victoria Chess (Greenwillow, 1979)

Alison's Zinnia by Anita Lobel (Greenwillow, 1990)

All Aboard ABC by Doug Magee and Robert Newman (Dutton, 1990)

Alligator Arrived With Apples: A Potluck Alphabet Feast by Crescent Dragonwagon (Macmillan, 1987)

Alligators All Around: An Alphabet by Maurice Sendak (HarperCollins, 1962)

All in the Woodland Early: An ABC Book by Jane Yolen (Collins, 1979)

Alphababies by Kim Golding (DK Publishing,1998)

Alphabatics by Suse MacDonald (Aladdin, 1992)

Alphabears: An ABC Book by Kathleen Hague (Holt, Rinehart & Winston, 1984)

The Alphabet From Z to A (With Much Confusion on the Way) by Judith Viorst (Atheneum, 1994)

An Alphabet of Animals by Christopher Wormell (Dial Books, 1990)

An Alphabet of Dinosaurs by Peter Dodson (Scholastic, 1995)

Alphabet Out Loud by Ruth Gembicki Bragg (Picture Book Studio, 1991)

Alphabet Puzzle by Jill Downie (Lothrop, Lee & Shepard, 1988)

Alphabet Soup by Kate Banks (Knopf, 1988)

Alphabet Soup by Abbie Zabar (Stewart, Tabori & Chang, 1990)

Alphabet Times Four: An International ABC by Ruth Brown (Dutton, 1991)

The Alphabet Tree by Leo Lionni (Pantheon, 1968)

AlphaTales Learning Library: 26 Paperback Books Plus Teaching Guide (Scholastic Teaching Resources, 2001)

Animal Alphabet by Bert Kitchen (Dial, 1984)

Animalia by Graeme Base (Viking Kestrel, 1986)

Anno's Alphabet: An Adventure in Imagination by Mitsumasa Anno (Crowell, 1975)

The Ark in the Attic: An Alphabet Adventure by Eileen Doolittle (D. R. Godine, 1987)

Ashanti to Zulu: African Traditions by Margaret Musgrove (Dial, 1976)

Aster Aardvark's Alphabet Adventures by Steven Kellogg (William Morrow, 1987)

Baseball ABC by Florence Cassen Mayers (Harry N. Abrams, 1994)

The Butterfly Alphabet by Kjell B. Sandved (Scholastic, 1996)

California A to Z by Dorothy Hines Weaver (Rising Moon, 1999)

Cat Alphabet by Metropolitan Museum of Art (Bulfinch, 1994)

Chicka Chicka Boom Boom by Bill Martin, Jr. and John Archambault (Simon & Schuster, 1989)

C Is for Curious: An ABC of Feelings by Woodleigh Hubbard (Chronicle Books, 1990)

City Seen From A to Z by Rachel Isadora (Greenwillow, 1983)

Clifford's ABC by Norman Bridwell (Scholastic, 1994)

Community Helpers From A to Z by Bobbie Kalman (Crabtree, 1998)

Crazy Alphabet by Lynn Cox (Orchard Books, 1992)

David McPhail's Animals A to Z by David McPhail (Scholastic, 1988)

The Desert Alphabet Book by Jerry Palotta (Charlesbridge, 1994)

The Dinosaur Alphabet by Jerry Palotta (Charlesbridge, 1991)

The Disappearing Alphabet by Richard Wilbur (Harcourt Brace, 1998)

Earth From A to Z by Bobbie Kalman and John Crossingham (Crabtree, 1999)

Eating the Alphabet: Fruits and Vegetables From A to Z by Lois Ehlert (Harcourt Brace Jovanovich, 1989)

Erni Cabat's Magical ABC Animals Around the Farm by Erni Cabat (Harbinger House, 1992)

The Extinct Alphabet Book by Jerry Palotta (Charlesbridge, 1993)

Farm Alphabet Book by Jane Miller (J. M. Dent, 1981)

A Farmer's Alphabet by Mary Azarian (D. R. Godine, 1981)

Firefighters A to Z by Chris L. Demarest (Margaret K. McElderry, 2000)

The Freshwater Alphabet Book by Jerry Palotta (Charlesbridge, 1996)

The Frog Alphabet Book by Jerry Palotta (Charlesbridge, 1990)

The Furry Alphabet Book by Jerry Palotta (Charlesbridge, 1990)

From Acorn to Zoo and Everything in Between in Alphabetical Order by Satoshi Kitamura (Farrar, Strauss, and Giroux, 1992)

From Letter to Letter by Terri Sloat (Dutton, 1989)

The Graphic Alphabet by David Pelletier (Orchard, 1996)

Geography From A to Z: A Picture Glossary by Jack Knowlton (Crowell, 1988)

Gretchen's ABC by Gretchen Dow Simpson (HarperCollins, 1991)

Gyo Fujikawa's A to Z Picture Book by Gyo Fujikawa (Grosset & Dunlap, 1974)

The Handmade Alphabet by Laura Rankin (Dial, 1991)

The Icky Bug Alphabet by Jerry Pallotta (Charlesbridge, 1986)

It Begins With an A by Stephanie Calmenson (Hyperion, 1993)

Jambo Means Hello: Swahili Alphabet Book by Muriel Feelings (Dial, 1974)

The Letters Are Lost by Lisa Campbell Ernst (Viking, 1996)

Mexico From A to Z by Bobbie Kalman and Jane Lewis (Crabtree, 1999)

Miss Spider's ABC by David Kirk (Scholastic, 1998)

The Monster Book of ABC Sounds by Alan Snow (Dial, 1991)

Museum Alphabet by Gisela Voss and Suwin Chan (Museum of Fine Arts, Boston 1995)

My Alphabet Animals Draw Along Book by Dixie Heath (Knight, 1993)

Pierrot's ABC Garden by Anita Lobel (Golden Books, 1992)

Pigs From A to Z by Arthur Geisert (Houghton Mifflin, 1986)

School From A to Z by Bobbie Kalman (Crabtree, 1999)

The Sesame Street ABC Book of Words by Harry McNaught (Random House/ Children's Television Workshop, 1988)

Texas Alphabet by James Rice (Pelican Publishing, 1988)

Tomorrow's Alphabet by George Shannon (Greenwillow, 1995)

26 Letters and 99 Cents by Tana Hoban (Greenwillow, 1988)

The Underwater Alphabet Book by Jerry Palotta (Charlesbridge, 1991)

United States from A to Z by Bobbie Kalman and Kate Calder (Crabtree, 1999)

Wild Animals of Africa ABC by Hope Ryden (Lodestar, 1989)

The Wildlife A-B-C: A Nature Alphabet Book by Jan Thornhill (Simon & Schuster Books for Young Readers, 1990)

The Yucky Reptile Alphabet Book by Jerry Palotta (Charlesbridge, 1989)

The Z Was Zapped by Chris Van Allsburg (Houghton Mifflin, 1987)

Aa•Bb•Cc•Aa•Bb•Cc•Aa•Bb•Cc•Aa•Bb•Cc•Aa•Bb•Cc

Bibliography

Adams, Marilyn Jager. *Beginning to Read: Thinking and Learning About Print.* Cambridge: The MIT Press, 1990.

Arena, John I., ed. *Building Handwriting Skills in Dyslexic Children.* San Rafael, California: Academic Therapy Publications, 1970.

Bear et al., *Words Their Way: Word Study for Phonics, Vocabulary, and Spelling Instruction.* Englewood Cliffs, New Jersey: Merrill/Prentice Hall, 1996.

Blevins, Wiley. *Phonics A–Z: A Practical Guide.* New York: Scholastic, 1998.